Investing for Beginners

A Casual Guide

Mark Freedman

Weird Candle Publishing

© 2024 Mark Freedman, Weird Candle Publishing. All rights reserved.

No part of this publication may be reproduced, distributed, or transmitted in any form or by any means, including photocopying, recording, or other electronic or mechanical methods, without the prior written permission of the publisher, except in the case of brief quotations embodied in critical reviews and certain other noncommercial uses permitted by copyright law. For permission requests, write to the publisher, addressed "Attention: Permissions Coordinator," at the address below.

Mark Freedman
Weird Candle Publishing
info@weirdcandle.com

Ordering Information:

Special discounts are available on quantity purchases by corporations, associations, and others. For details, contact the publisher at the email address above.

Publishing

Disclaimer:
The views and opinions expressed in this book are those of the author and do not necessarily reflect the official policy or position of any agency or organization. The information provided in this book is for informational purposes only and should not be considered financial advice. Readers are encouraged to conduct their own research and consult with a qualified financial advisor before making any investment decisions. The author and publisher are not responsible for any losses or damages that may result from following the information provided in this book.

ISBN: 9798332322419
Printed in the United States of America
First Printing, 2024

To Lorri

You are my everything.

Chapter 1: Introduction..7
   Why Investing Matters... 7
   My Personal Journey with Investing.................................. 8
   What to Expect from This Book.. 8
Chapter 2: Getting Started... 11
   Understanding Your Financial Situation........................... 11
   Setting Financial Goals.. 12
   The Magic of Compound Interest................................... 12
   Taking Action... 13
   Summary.. 14
Chapter 3: Investment Basics... 15
   Stocks, Bonds, and Other Investment Types..................15
   Risk vs. Reward.. 16
   Summary... 19
Chapter 4: How to Invest..21
   Opening an Investment Account......................................21
   Choosing Between DIY and Financial Advisors.............. 23
   Summary.. 26
Chapter 5: Building Your Portfolio..27
   Asset Allocation: Finding the Right Mix........................... 27
   Example Portfolios...28
   Long-term vs. Short-term Investments............................ 31
   Summary.. 33
Chapter 6: Investment Strategies.. 35
   Value Investing.. 35
   Growth Investing..36
   Dividend Investing... 38
   Combining Strategies.. 39
   Summary.. 39
Chapter 7: Common Investment Mistakes............................ 41
   Emotional Investing... 41
   Timing the Market.. 42
   Ignoring Costs..43

Chasing Performance... 45
Overlooking the Importance of Diversification...................... 46
Summary.. 47
Chapter 8: Advanced Topics... 49
Tax-Advantaged Accounts... 49
Real Estate Investing.. 52
Investing in Cryptocurrencies... 54
Summary.. 56
Chapter 9: Staying Informed.. 59
Continuing Your Investment Education.................................. 59
Resources and Tools.. 61
Following the Market News.. 62
Engage with Financial Communities...................................... 63
Attend Conferences and Seminars.. 63
Mentorship and Professional Advice..................................... 63
Summary.. 64
Chapter 10: Conclusion.. 65
Recap of Key Points... 65
Encouragement for the Future... 68
Appendix: Beginner-Friendly Investment Sites and Tools... 69
Investment Platforms.. 69
Financial News and Research Tools...................................... 70
Educational Resources... 71
Budgeting and Financial Planning Tools................................ 72
Index... **73**

Chapter 1: Introduction

Hey there! Welcome to your first step into the world of investing. If you're feeling a bit overwhelmed or intimidated, don't worry—you're definitely not alone. I was in your shoes once, not too long ago. But with some patience and persistence, I managed to navigate my way through, and now, I'm here to help you do the same.

Why Investing Matters

Why does investing matter, you ask? Well, it's like planting a tree. The sooner you start, the sooner you'll enjoy the shade. Investing isn't just for the wealthy or the finance geeks; it's for anyone who wants to build a better financial future. Whether you're saving for retirement, a down payment on a house, or just trying to grow your savings, investing is a key tool in your financial toolbox.

Here are a few reasons why investing is crucial:

- **Building Wealth:** Investing helps you grow your money over time, allowing you to build wealth and achieve your financial goals.
- **Beating Inflation:** Inflation erodes the purchasing power of your money. By investing, you can earn returns that outpace inflation, preserving and growing your wealth.
- **Achieving Financial Goals:** Whether it's buying a home, funding your child's education, or planning for retirement, investing can help you reach your financial milestones.
- **Financial Security:** Investing provides an additional income stream and helps you build a financial safety net for emergencies or unexpected expenses.

My Personal Journey with Investing

Let me share a bit about my journey. I've been involved in the tech world for nearly 40 years, but it wasn't until later in life that I truly started paying attention to investing. Like many, I made some mistakes along the way, but I learned a lot. Now, with some experience under my belt, I want to pass on those lessons to you.

I started out like most people, putting a little money into a savings account and thinking I was doing enough. But as I learned more about personal finance, I realized that saving alone wouldn't get me where I wanted to be. I needed to make my money work for me, and that's when I turned to investing.

My first foray into investing was through a retirement account at work. It was simple enough: contribute a portion of my salary and let the professionals handle the rest. Over time, I saw my balance grow, not just from my contributions but also from the returns on my investments. This was the power of compound interest at work.

But I wanted to learn more and take control of my financial future. So, I started reading books, attending seminars, and even dabbling in DIY investing. I made some good decisions and, admittedly, some bad ones too. But each experience taught me valuable lessons that I'm eager to share with you.

What to Expect from This Book

This book is designed to be your go-to guide for getting started with investing. We'll cover everything you need to know, from understanding your financial situation to building a diversified portfolio. Along the way, I'll share practical tips and personal anecdotes to make the concepts more relatable and easier to understand.

Here's a sneak peek of what's in store:

- **Chapter 2: Getting Started** – We'll lay the groundwork by helping you assess your financial situation and set clear, achievable goals. We'll also introduce you to the magic of compound interest and how it can supercharge your investments.
- **Chapter 3: Investment Basics** – You'll learn about different types of investments, the relationship between risk and reward, and the importance of diversification.
- **Chapter 4: How to Invest** – We'll guide you through the process of opening an investment account, choosing between DIY investing and financial advisors, and understanding investment fees.
- **Chapter 5: Building Your Portfolio** – Discover how to allocate your assets, rebalance your portfolio, and decide between long-term and short-term investments.
- **Chapter 6: Investment Strategies** – Explore popular investment strategies like value investing, growth investing, and dividend investing.
- **Chapter 7: Common Investment Mistakes** – Learn about common pitfalls to avoid, such as emotional investing, trying to time the market, and ignoring costs.
- **Chapter 8: Advanced Topics** – Delve into tax-advantaged accounts, real estate investing, and cryptocurrencies.
- **Chapter 9: Staying Informed** – Find out how to continue your investment education, stay updated on market news, and use resources and tools to your advantage.
- **Chapter 10: Conclusion** – We'll recap the key points and offer some encouragement for your future as an investor.

Chapter 2: Getting Started

Before you start throwing your money into the stock market, it's crucial to understand where you stand financially. Take a good look at your income, expenses, and debts. This might seem tedious, but trust me, knowing your financial health is the foundation of successful investing.

Understanding Your Financial Situation

Start by creating a detailed budget. Track your monthly income and expenses, including all those little things that add up. There are many budgeting tools and apps available that can make this process easier. Tiller Money[1], YNAB (You Need A Budget)[2], and Empower[3] are popular options. Once you have a clear picture, you can see how much money you have left to invest each month.

Here's a simple way to get started with budgeting:

1. **List Your Income:** Include all sources of income such as salary, freelance work, rental income, etc.
2. **Track Your Expenses:** Divide your expenses into categories like housing, utilities, groceries, transportation, entertainment, and savings.
3. **Analyze Your Spending:** Identify areas where you can cut back. Maybe those daily coffee runs add up more than you realized.
4. **Calculate Your Surplus or Deficit:** Subtract your total expenses from your total income. The amount left over is your potential investment fund.

---

[1] https://tillerhq.com
[2] https://ynab.com
[3] https://empower.com

By understanding your financial situation, you can make informed decisions about how much you can afford to invest without impacting your daily living and emergency savings.

Setting Financial Goals

Next up, let's talk about goals. What are you investing for? Retirement? Buying a house? Traveling the world? Having clear goals helps you determine your investment strategy and stay motivated. Write down your goals, both short-term and long-term, and keep them in mind as you start your investment journey.

Here are a few tips for setting financial goals:

- **Be Specific:** Instead of saying, "I want to save for retirement," specify how much you need and by when. For example, "I want to save $500,000 for retirement by age 65."
- **Make Them Measurable:** Ensure you can track your progress. This might mean setting monthly or yearly targets.
- **Set Realistic Goals:** While it's good to aim high, your goals should be achievable based on your current financial situation.
- **Prioritize:** Rank your goals in order of importance. This helps you allocate your resources effectively.

Remember, your goals will shape your investment strategy. Short-term goals might require more conservative investments, while long-term goals can afford more risk.

The Magic of Compound Interest

And don't forget the magic word: compound interest. It's the secret sauce that makes your money grow exponentially over time. Imagine your investments earning returns, and those returns earning returns. It's like a snowball effect, and the earlier you start, the bigger the snowball gets.

Here's how compound interest works:

1. **Initial Investment:** Suppose you invest $1,000 at an annual interest rate of 5%.
2. **Year 1:** After one year, your investment grows to $1,050 (your initial $1,000 plus $50 in interest).
3. **Year 2:** In the second year, you earn interest not just on your initial $1,000, but also on the $50 interest from the first year. So, your investment grows to $1,102.50.

Over time, this compounding effect can lead to significant growth in your investments. The key takeaway? Start investing as early as possible to maximize the benefits of compound interest.

Taking Action

Now that you understand your financial situation, have set your goals, and grasp the power of compound interest, it's time to take action. Here are some steps to get started:

- **Pay Off High-Interest Debt:** Before you start investing, it's usually wise to pay off any high-interest debt, like credit cards. The interest on these debts can be much higher than the returns you'd earn from investing. We did this after accumulating a lot of debt starting from when we had to pay for formula and diapers. It took about 15 years or so, but when we paid it off – wow, what a relief! And we've avoided it since.
- **Build an Emergency Fund:** Make sure you have an emergency fund to cover 3-6 months of living expenses. This fund acts as a safety net, so you don't have to sell investments during a financial emergency.

- **Determine Your Investment Amount:** Based on your budget, decide how much you can invest each month. Consistency is key, even if you start small.
- **Educate Yourself:** Continue learning about investing. Books, podcasts, online courses, and financial blogs are great resources. The more you know, the more confident you'll feel.

Summary

By understanding your financial situation, setting clear goals, leveraging the power of compound interest, and taking concrete steps, you're well on your way to starting your investment journey. In the next chapter, we'll dive into the basics of different types of investments and how to balance risk and reward. Stay tuned!

Chapter 3: Investment Basics

Alright, let's get to the nitty-gritty. There are many ways to invest your money, but the most common types are stocks and bonds. Understanding these basics is crucial to making informed decisions and building a solid investment strategy.

Stocks, Bonds, and Other Investment Types

Stocks

Stocks represent ownership in a company. When you buy a stock, you own a piece of that company, and your wealth grows as the company grows. Stocks can offer high returns, but they also come with higher risk. The value of a stock can fluctuate based on the company's performance and broader market conditions.

Example: If you buy 100 shares of Apple Inc. (AAPL) at $150 each, and the stock price rises to $200, your investment will grow from $15,000 to $20,000. However, if the stock price falls to $100, your investment will decrease to $10,000.

Bonds

Bonds are essentially loans you give to companies or governments. In return, you receive regular interest payments and get your principal back at the end of the bond's term. Bonds are generally considered safer than stocks because they provide steady income and are less volatile. However, they typically offer lower returns.

Example: If you buy a $1,000 bond with a 5% annual interest rate, you'll receive $50 each year until the bond matures. At maturity, you'll get your $1,000 back.

Other Investment Types

Besides stocks and bonds, there are other investment vehicles you might consider:

- **Mutual Funds:** These are pools of money from many investors, managed by a professional. Mutual funds invest in a diversified portfolio of stocks, bonds, or other assets. They offer diversification and professional management but come with management fees.
- **Exchange-Traded Funds (ETFs):** Similar to mutual funds, ETFs are collections of stocks or bonds. They trade on stock exchanges, providing the flexibility of buying and selling shares throughout the day. ETFs typically have lower fees than mutual funds.
- **Real Estate:** Investing in property can provide rental income and potential appreciation in value. You can invest directly in real estate or through Real Estate Investment Trusts (REITs), which are companies that own and manage properties.
- **Cryptocurrencies:** Digital currencies like Bitcoin and Ethereum are gaining popularity. They offer high potential returns but come with significant risk and volatility. Investing in cryptocurrencies requires careful research and understanding of the market.

Risk vs. Reward

Investing is all about balancing risk and reward. Higher potential returns usually come with higher risk. The key is to find a balance that matches your risk tolerance and financial goals.

Understanding Risk Tolerance

Risk tolerance refers to your ability and willingness to endure market fluctuations. Factors influencing risk tolerance include your financial situation, investment goals, time horizon, and personality.

- **Conservative Investors:** Prefer stability and are willing to accept lower returns to avoid significant losses. They might focus on bonds and dividend-paying stocks.
- **Moderate Investors:** Comfortable with some risk and fluctuations in exchange for higher returns. They might have a balanced mix of stocks and bonds.
- **Aggressive Investors:** Willing to accept higher risk for the potential of substantial returns. They often invest heavily in stocks and other high-risk assets.

Evaluating Potential Rewards

When evaluating potential investments, consider the historical performance, projected growth, and the underlying factors driving those returns. While past performance doesn't guarantee future results, it provides insight into how the investment might behave.

Example

- **Stocks:** Historically, the U.S. stock market has averaged annual returns of about 7-10% after inflation. However, individual stock performance can vary widely.
- **Bonds:** Government bonds might offer annual returns of 2-3%, while corporate bonds might offer 4-6%, depending on their credit risk.

Diversification: Don't Put All Your Eggs in One Basket

Diversification is a key strategy for managing risk. It involves spreading your investments across different asset classes, industries, and geographic regions to reduce exposure to any single investment's risk.

Benefits of Diversification

- **Risk Reduction:** Diversification helps mitigate the impact of a poor-performing investment on your overall portfolio. If one asset class or industry suffers, others might perform well, balancing your returns.
- **Smoother Returns:** A diversified portfolio is less likely to experience extreme volatility, providing more stable returns over time.
- **Opportunity for Growth:** By investing in a variety of assets, you can take advantage of growth opportunities in different markets and sectors.

How to Diversify

- **Asset Allocation:** Determine the right mix of stocks, bonds, real estate, and other assets based on your risk tolerance and goals. For example, a conservative investor might have 60% in bonds and 40% in stocks, while an aggressive investor might have 80% in stocks and 20% in bonds.
- **Industry Diversification:** Invest in different industries to avoid overexposure to any single sector. For instance, instead of investing only in tech stocks, include healthcare, finance, consumer goods, and other sectors.
- **Geographic Diversification:** Spread your investments across different countries and regions to reduce exposure to economic and political risks in any single market.

Example Portfolio

- 40% U.S. Stocks
- 20% International Stocks
- 20% Bonds
- 10% Real Estate (REITs)
- 10% Cash or Cash Equivalents

Summary

Understanding the basics of stocks, bonds, and other investment types is essential for building a solid foundation. Balancing risk and reward according to your risk tolerance and goals helps you make informed decisions. Diversification reduces risk and increases the potential for stable returns. With these fundamentals in place, you're ready to start building your investment portfolio.

In the next chapter, we'll guide you through the practical steps of how to invest, from opening an investment account to choosing between DIY investing and financial advisors. Stay tuned!

Chapter 4: How to Invest

So, you're ready to start investing. Great! This chapter will guide you through the practical steps of how to invest, from opening an investment account to choosing between DIY investing and financial advisors, and understanding investment fees.

Opening an Investment Account

The first step in your investment journey is to open an investment account. There are different types of accounts you can choose from, each with its own benefits and purposes.

Types of Investment Accounts

Brokerage Accounts: These are standard investment accounts that allow you to buy and sell a variety of investments, including stocks, bonds, mutual funds, and ETFs. They offer flexibility and accessibility but come with no tax advantages.

Retirement Accounts: These accounts are specifically designed to help you save for retirement. They offer tax advantages that can help your investments grow more efficiently. Common types include:

- **Traditional IRA:** Contributions are tax-deductible, and investments grow tax-deferred until you withdraw them in retirement.
- **Roth IRA:** Contributions are made with after-tax dollars, but your investments grow tax-free, and withdrawals in retirement are also tax-free.
- **401(k):** Employer-sponsored retirement plans that may include employer matching contributions. Contributions

are tax-deferred, and investments grow tax-free until withdrawal.

Choosing a Brokerage

When selecting a brokerage, consider the following factors:

- **Fees and Commissions:** Look for brokerages with low fees and commissions. Many now offer commission-free trading for stocks and ETFs.
- **Investment Options:** Ensure the brokerage offers a wide range of investment options, including stocks, bonds, mutual funds, and ETFs.
- **User Experience:** The platform should be easy to use and offer helpful tools and resources for investors.
- **Customer Service:** Reliable customer support is crucial, especially if you're new to investing.

Some popular online brokerages include:

- Vanguard[4]
- Fidelity[5]
- Charles Schwab[6]
- Robinhood[7]
- E*TRADE[8]

Opening Your Account

To open an investment account, you'll typically need to provide:

- **Personal Information:** Name, address, Social Security number, and employment details.

---

[4] https://vanguard.com
[5] https://fidelity.com
[6] https://schwab.com
[7] https://robinhood.com
[8] https://us.etrade.com

- **Financial Information:** Your income, net worth, and investment experience.
- **Funding Source:** Link a bank account to transfer funds into your investment account.

Once your account is open and funded, you're ready to start investing!

Choosing Between DIY and Financial Advisors

Next, decide if you want to manage your investments yourself (DIY) or hire a financial advisor. Both approaches have their pros and cons.

DIY Investing

Pros

- **Lower Costs:** You save on advisor fees, which can be significant over time.
- **Control:** You have complete control over your investment decisions.
- **Learning Opportunity:** Managing your own investments can be a great way to learn about the market.

Cons

- **Time-Consuming:** Researching and managing investments takes time and effort.
- **Knowledge Required:** You need to educate yourself and stay informed about the market.

Financial Advisors

Pros

- **Expertise:** Advisors bring professional knowledge and experience to your investment strategy.
- **Personalized Advice:** They provide tailored advice based on your financial situation and goals.
- **Time-Saving:** Advisors handle the research and management of your investments.

Cons

- **Higher Costs:** Advisors charge fees, which can eat into your returns. These can be flat fees, hourly rates, or a percentage of assets under management (AUM).
- **Potential Bias:** Some advisors may have conflicts of interest, especially if they earn commissions on the products they recommend.

Types of Financial Advisors

- **Robo-Advisors:** Automated platforms that use algorithms to manage your investments based on your risk tolerance and goals. They offer low fees and minimal human interaction. Examples include Betterment, Wealthfront, and Vanguard Personal Advisor Services.
- **Traditional Financial Advisors:** Human advisors who provide personalized advice and manage your investments. They offer comprehensive financial planning but at a higher cost.
- **Hybrid Advisors:** A combination of robo-advisors and human advisors, offering a balance of automated

management and personalized advice. Examples include Empower[9] and Schwab Intelligent Portfolios[10].

Understanding Investment Fees

Investment fees can significantly impact your returns over time, so it's essential to understand the costs associated with investing.

Common Investment Fees

- **Expense Ratios:** These are annual fees charged by mutual funds and ETFs, expressed as a percentage of assets under management[11]. Lower expense ratios mean more of your money stays invested.
- **Commissions:** Fees charged for buying and selling securities. Many brokerages now offer commission-free trading for stocks and ETFs.
- **Account Fees:** Some brokerages charge fees for maintaining your account, especially for retirement accounts like IRAs.
- **Advisor Fees:** If you use a financial advisor, they may charge flat fees, hourly rates, or a percentage of your assets under management (AUM).

Example: If you invest $10,000 in a mutual fund with a 1% expense ratio, you'll pay $100 annually in fees. Over time, this can add up, reducing your overall returns.

Minimizing Fees

- **Choose Low-Cost Funds:** Look for mutual funds and ETFs with low expense ratios.

---

[9] https://empower.com
[10] https://schwab.com
[11] https://www.investopedia.com/terms/a/aum.asp

- **Consider Commission-Free Brokerages:** Many online brokerages offer commission-free trading for stocks and ETFs.
- **Avoid Frequent Trading:** Frequent buying and selling can lead to higher commissions and potential tax implications.
- **Be Aware of Advisor Fees:** Understand how your advisor is compensated and look for fee-only advisors who do not earn commissions on the products they recommend.

Summary

Opening an investment account, choosing between DIY investing and financial advisors, and understanding investment fees are crucial steps in your investment journey. By making informed decisions and minimizing costs, you can set yourself up for success. In the next chapter, we'll explore how to build your investment portfolio, including asset allocation and rebalancing strategies. Stay tuned!

Chapter 5: Building Your Portfolio

Now that you have an account, it's time to build your portfolio. This chapter will guide you through the process of asset allocation, rebalancing, and choosing between long-term and short-term investments.

Asset Allocation: Finding the Right Mix

Asset allocation is about deciding how to divide your money among different types of investments. This depends on your risk tolerance, goals, and time horizon. A well-balanced portfolio can help you achieve your financial objectives while managing risk.

Understanding Asset Classes

- **Stocks:** Represent ownership in a company. They offer high growth potential but come with higher risk. Stocks are ideal for long-term growth.
- **Bonds:** Loans to companies or governments that pay regular interest. They provide more stable returns with lower risk. Bonds are suitable for income and capital preservation.
- **Cash and Cash Equivalents:** Include savings accounts, money market funds, and Treasury bills. They offer the least risk but the lowest returns. Cash is essential for liquidity and emergency funds.
- **Real Estate:** Investments in property or REITs (Real Estate Investment Trusts). Real estate can provide rental income and potential appreciation.

- **Commodities:** Include gold, silver, oil, and agricultural products. Commodities can hedge against inflation but are highly volatile.
- **Alternative Investments:** Include hedge funds[12], private equity[13], and collectibles. These are typically for more advanced investors seeking diversification beyond traditional assets.

Determining Your Asset Allocation

Your asset allocation should reflect your risk tolerance, investment goals, and time horizon. Here are some common strategies:

Conservative

Suitable for risk-averse investors with a shorter time horizon or those nearing retirement. Focuses on capital preservation with lower risk.

Moderate

Balances growth and stability. Suitable for investors with a medium time horizon and moderate risk tolerance.

Aggressive

Suitable for younger investors or those with a long time horizon who can tolerate higher volatility for potential higher returns.

Example Portfolios

- **Conservative Portfolio:** 30% U.S. stocks, 10% international stocks, 50% bonds, 10% cash.

---

[12] https://www.investopedia.com/terms/h/hedgefund.asp
[13] https://www.investopedia.com/terms/p/privateequity.asp

- **Moderate Portfolio:** 40% U.S. stocks, 20% international stocks, 30% bonds, 10% cash.
- **Aggressive Portfolio:** 60% U.S. stocks, 20% international stocks, 10% bonds, 10% cash.

Adjusting Over Time

Your asset allocation should evolve as your circumstances change. For example, as you approach retirement, you might shift from an aggressive to a more conservative allocation to protect your savings.

Rebalancing: Keeping Your Portfolio Healthy

Rebalancing involves adjusting your portfolio periodically to maintain your desired asset allocation. Over time, market fluctuations can cause your portfolio to drift from its target allocation.

Why Rebalance?

- **Maintain Risk Level:** Rebalancing helps you maintain your desired risk level. If stocks perform well and their value increases, your portfolio might become more aggressive than intended.
- **Buy Low, Sell High:** Rebalancing involves selling high-performing assets and buying underperforming ones, adhering to the principle of buying low and selling high[14].
- **Discipline:** Regular rebalancing promotes disciplined investing and prevents emotional decision-making.

---

[14] https://www.investopedia.com/articles/investing/081415/look-buy-low-sell-high-strategy.asp

How to Rebalance

1. **Set a Schedule:** Rebalance your portfolio at regular intervals, such as annually or semi-annually. Alternatively, rebalance when your asset allocation deviates significantly from your target (e.g., by 5-10%).
2. **Review Your Allocation:** Compare your current allocation to your target allocation. Identify which assets are over or underweight.
3. **Adjust Holdings:** Sell overweight assets and buy underweight assets to realign your portfolio with your target allocation. Consider transaction costs and tax implications when making adjustments.

Example

Let's say you start with a portfolio that has $6,000 in stocks and $4,000 in bonds, maintaining a 60% stocks and 40% bonds allocation.

Initial Allocation:

- Stocks: $6,000 (60%)
- Bonds: $4,000 (40%)

After a year, due to market performance, the value of your stocks might increase to $7,000 while the value of your bonds increases to $4,200.

New Allocation:

- Stocks: $7,000
- Bonds: $4,200
- Total Portfolio Value: $11,200

To find the new percentages:

- Stocks: $7,000 / $11,200 ≈ 62.5%

- Bonds: $4,200 / $11,200 ≈ 37.5%

This shift means your portfolio is now 62.5% in stocks and 37.5% in bonds, deviating from your target allocation of 60% stocks and 40% bonds.

To rebalance back to your target allocation, you would sell some stocks and buy bonds to bring the portfolio back to the original 60/40 split.

Target Allocation:

- 60% of $11,200 in stocks: 0.60 * $11,200 = $6,720
- 40% of $11,200 in bonds: 0.40 * $11,200 = $4,480

Rebalancing:

- Current stocks: $7,000
- Target stocks: $6,720
- Sell: $7,000 - $6,720 = $280 worth of stocks
- Current bonds: $4,200
- Target bonds: $4,480
- Buy: $4,480 - $4,200 = $280 worth of bonds

By selling $280 worth of stocks and buying $280 worth of bonds, you realign your portfolio back to the target 60/40 allocation.

This way, the portfolio maintains the desired risk level and investment strategy.

Long-term vs. Short-term Investments

Consider the time frame for your investments. Long-term and short-term investments serve different purposes and should be selected based on your goals and time horizon.

Long-term Investments

Long-term investments are held for several years or decades. They are ideal for goals like retirement, funding a child's education, or building wealth. Long-term investments can afford to weather market volatility and benefit from compound growth.

Examples

- **Stocks:** Historically, stocks have provided higher returns over the long term. They are suitable for investors with a time horizon of 10 years or more.
- **Real Estate:** Property investments can appreciate over time and provide rental income. Real estate is typically a long-term commitment.
- **Retirement Accounts:** Contributions to IRAs or 401(k)s are intended for long-term growth and retirement savings.

Short-term Investments

Short-term investments are held for a few months to a few years. They are suitable for goals like buying a car, funding a vacation, or building an emergency fund. Short-term investments prioritize capital preservation and liquidity.

Examples

- **Cash and Cash Equivalents:** Savings accounts, money market funds, and Treasury bills provide safety and easy access to funds.
- **Short-term Bonds:** Bonds with maturities of less than five years offer stability and income.
- **Certificates of Deposit (CDs):** Fixed-term savings accounts that pay interest. CDs with short maturities are suitable for short-term goals.

Balancing Long-term and Short-term Investments

Your portfolio should include a mix of long-term and short-term investments based on your goals. For example, you might allocate a portion of your portfolio to stocks for long-term growth while keeping some cash or short-term bonds for immediate needs.

Example Allocation

- **Long-term:** 70% stocks, 20% bonds
- **Short-term:** 10% cash and cash equivalents

Summary

Building your portfolio involves determining the right asset allocation, regularly rebalancing to maintain your target mix, and balancing long-term and short-term investments based on your goals. A well-constructed portfolio can help you achieve your financial objectives while managing risk. In the next chapter, we'll explore different investment strategies, including value investing, growth investing, and dividend investing. Stay tuned!

Chapter 6: Investment Strategies

Different strategies can help you achieve your financial goals. In this chapter, we'll explore some popular investment strategies: value investing, growth investing, and dividend investing. Each strategy has its unique approach and benefits, so you can choose the one that best aligns with your goals and risk tolerance.

Value Investing

Value investing involves buying undervalued stocks that you believe will increase in value over time. It's like finding hidden gems in the market. Value investors look for companies whose stock prices don't fully reflect their intrinsic value, offering a margin of safety.

Key Principles

- **Intrinsic Value:** This is the true worth of a company based on its fundamentals, such as earnings, dividends, and growth potential. Value investors seek stocks trading below their intrinsic value.
- **Margin of Safety:** By purchasing stocks at a discount to their intrinsic value, investors have a buffer against potential losses.
- **Fundamental Analysis:** Value investors analyze financial statements, earnings reports, and other data to assess a company's true worth.

How to Implement Value Investing

1. **Identify Undervalued Stocks:** Look for stocks with low price-to-earnings[15] (P/E) ratios, price-to-book[16] (P/B) ratios, and strong fundamentals.
2. **Research the Company:** Analyze the company's financial health, competitive position, management quality, and growth prospects.
3. **Calculate Intrinsic Value:** Use valuation models[17] like discounted cash flow[18] (DCF) analysis to estimate the stock's intrinsic value.
4. **Buy and Hold:** Purchase undervalued stocks and hold them until they reach or exceed their intrinsic value.

Example

If a stock is trading at $50, but your analysis shows its intrinsic value is $70, you might consider it a good value investment. By buying the stock at $50, you have a margin of safety of $20.

Growth Investing

Growth investing focuses on companies with strong potential for future growth. These companies might not be profitable yet, but they're expected to grow rapidly. This strategy can offer high returns but comes with higher risk.

---

[15] https://www.investopedia.com/terms/p/price-earningsratio.asp

[16] https://www.investopedia.com/investing/using-price-to-book-ratio-evaluate-companies

[17] https://www.investopedia.com/articles/fundamental-analysis/11/choosing-valuation-methods.asp

[18] https://www.investopedia.com/terms/d/dcf.asp

Key Principles

- **Revenue and Earnings Growth:** Growth investors look for companies with high revenue and earnings growth rates, indicating strong potential for future expansion.
- **Market Trends:** Identify industries and sectors with significant growth potential, such as technology, healthcare, and renewable energy.
- **Innovation and Competitive Advantage:** Invest in companies with innovative products, services, or business models that provide a competitive edge.

How to Implement Growth Investing

1. **Identify Growth Stocks:** Look for companies with high growth rates, strong revenue and earnings growth, and positive market sentiment[19].
2. **Analyze Growth Potential:** Evaluate the company's growth drivers, such as new products, market expansion, and technological advancements.
3. **Monitor Financial Health:** Ensure the company has a solid financial foundation to support its growth, including manageable debt levels and sufficient cash flow.
4. **Invest for the Long Term:** Growth stocks can be volatile in the short term, so be prepared to hold them for several years to realize their full potential.

Example

If a tech startup is growing its revenue by 30% annually and expanding into new markets, it might be a promising growth investment. Despite potential short-term volatility, the long-term growth prospects could lead to substantial returns.

---

[19] https://www.investopedia.com/terms/m/marketsentiment.asp

Dividend Investing

Dividend investing involves buying stocks that pay regular dividends. These companies distribute part of their profits to shareholders, providing a steady income stream. It's a great strategy for those seeking regular income and stability.

Key Principles

- **Dividend Yield:** The annual dividend payment divided by the stock price, expressed as a percentage. Higher yields provide more income but can indicate higher risk.
- **Dividend Payout Ratio:** The percentage of earnings paid out as dividends. A sustainable payout ratio ensures the company can maintain and grow its dividends.
- **Dividend Growth:** Look for companies with a history of increasing dividends over time, indicating financial strength and commitment to shareholders.

How to Implement Dividend Investing

1. **Identify Dividend Stocks:** Look for companies with a history of paying and increasing dividends. Utilities, consumer staples, and financials are common sectors for dividend stocks.
2. **Analyze Dividend Sustainability:** Evaluate the company's earnings, cash flow, and payout ratio to ensure it can sustain and grow its dividends.
3. **Build a Diversified Portfolio:** Diversify across different sectors and industries to reduce risk and ensure a stable income stream.
4. **Reinvest Dividends:** Consider reinvesting your dividends to compound your returns over time.

Example

If you invest in a company that pays a 4% annual dividend and reinvest those dividends, your investment will grow faster due to the power of compounding. For example, a $10,000 investment with a 4% dividend yield will generate $400 in dividends annually. By reinvesting those dividends, you'll buy more shares, increasing your future dividend payments.

Combining Strategies

You don't have to stick to just one strategy. Many investors combine value, growth, and dividend investing to create a balanced portfolio. For example, you might allocate a portion of your portfolio to high-growth tech stocks, stable dividend-paying utilities, and undervalued [blue-chip companies](https://www.investopedia.com/terms/b/bluechip.asp)[20].

Example Portfolio

- **40% Growth Stocks:** High-growth companies in technology, healthcare, and renewable energy.
- **30% Value Stocks:** Undervalued companies with strong fundamentals and potential for price appreciation.
- **30% Dividend Stocks:** Stable companies with a history of paying and increasing dividends.

Summary

Understanding different investment strategies like value investing, growth investing, and dividend investing helps you tailor your approach to your financial goals and risk tolerance. By combining strategies, you can create a diversified portfolio that balances growth, income, and stability. In the next chapter, we'll explore common investment mistakes and how to avoid them. Stay tuned!

---

[20] https://www.investopedia.com/terms/b/bluechip.asp

Chapter 7: Common Investment Mistakes

Avoiding common pitfalls can save you a lot of headaches and money. In this chapter, we'll explore some of the most frequent investment mistakes and how to avoid them. Understanding these traps can help you become a more disciplined and successful investor.

Emotional Investing

Investing based on emotions can lead to poor decisions. It's easy to get caught up in the excitement of a booming market or the fear of a downturn. Emotional investing often results in buying high and selling low, the opposite of what you should be doing.

Common Emotional Traps

- **Fear of Missing Out (FOMO):** Jumping into a hot stock or trend because everyone else is doing it. This can lead to buying at peak prices.
- **Panic Selling:** Selling investments during market downturns out of fear, locking in losses rather than waiting for a recovery.
- **Overconfidence:** Believing you can time the market or pick the next big winner consistently, leading to excessive risk-taking.

How to Avoid Emotional Investing

- **Have a Plan:** Develop a long-term investment strategy based on your goals and risk tolerance. Stick to it, even during market volatility.

- **Stay Informed:** Educate yourself about the market and your investments. Understanding why you invested in something can help you stay calm during market swings.
- **Limit News Consumption:** Constant exposure to market news can amplify emotional reactions. Limit your news intake to avoid making impulsive decisions. This is one I need to work at.
- **Use Automation:** Consider using automated investment tools or setting up automatic contributions to your investment accounts to stay disciplined.

Example

During the 2008 financial crisis, many investors panicked and sold their stocks at a loss. Those who stayed invested or even bought more stocks at lower prices eventually saw significant gains as the market recovered.

Timing the Market

Trying to predict market movements and time your investments perfectly is nearly impossible. Even the experts get it wrong. Instead, focus on long-term investing and ignore short-term market noise.

Why Timing the Market Fails

- **Market Unpredictability:** Financial markets are influenced by countless factors, making it extremely difficult to predict short-term movements accurately.
- **Emotional Decisions:** Timing the market often involves reacting to emotions, which can lead to buying high and selling low.
- **Missed Opportunities:** Staying out of the market during downturns means missing potential rebounds and gains.

Better Strategies

- **Dollar-Cost Averaging:** Invest a fixed amount regularly, regardless of market conditions. This strategy reduces the impact of volatility and removes the need to time the market.
- **Long-Term Focus:** Keep your investments for the long haul. Historical data shows that the market tends to go up over time, despite short-term fluctuations.
- **Diversification:** Spread your investments across different asset classes to reduce risk and smooth out returns.

Example

If you had invested $10,000 in the S&P 500 in 1980 and left it alone, your investment would be worth significantly more today (e.g., approximately $728,900 in 2024!), despite multiple market crashes and corrections. Trying to time the market would likely have resulted in missing some of the best days, reducing your overall returns.

Ignoring Costs

Investment fees and taxes can significantly impact your returns. Paying attention to costs and minimizing them whenever possible is crucial for maximizing your gains.

Types of Investment Costs

- **Expense Ratios:** Annual fees charged by mutual funds and ETFs, expressed as a percentage of assets under management. Lower expense ratios mean more of your money stays invested.
- **Commissions:** Fees charged for buying and selling securities. Many brokerages now offer commission-free trading for stocks and ETFs.

- **Account Fees:** Some brokerages charge fees for maintaining your account, especially for retirement accounts like IRAs.
- **Advisor Fees:** Fees charged by financial advisors, which can be flat fees, hourly rates, or a percentage of assets under management (AUM).
- **Taxes:** Capital gains taxes on profits from the sale of investments and taxes on dividends and interest income.

How to Minimize Costs

- **Choose Low-Cost Funds:** Look for mutual funds and ETFs with low expense ratios. Index funds often have lower fees than actively managed funds.
- **Use Commission-Free Brokerages:** Many online brokerages offer commission-free trading for stocks and ETFs. Take advantage of these platforms.
- **Avoid Frequent Trading:** Frequent buying and selling can lead to higher commissions and tax implications. Adopt a buy-and-hold strategy to minimize these costs.
- **Be Tax-Efficient:** Use tax-advantaged accounts like IRAs and 401(k)s to defer or avoid taxes. Consider tax-efficient investments and strategies to reduce your tax burden.

Example

If you invest $10,000 in a mutual fund with a 1% expense ratio, you'll pay $100 annually in fees. Over 30 years, these fees can add up significantly, reducing your overall returns. Choosing a fund with a 0.1% expense ratio would save you a substantial amount over time.

Chasing Performance

Investors often chase the latest hot stock or fund based on recent performance. This behavior can lead to buying high and missing out on future gains.

Why Chasing Performance is a Mistake

- **Reversion to the Mean:** High-performing investments often revert to their average performance over time. Buying after a strong run can result in lower future returns.
- **Lack of Diversification:** Focusing on top performers can lead to an unbalanced portfolio, increasing risk.
- **Overlooking Fundamentals:** Chasing performance might lead you to invest in companies or funds without considering their underlying fundamentals.

Better Approaches

- **Diversified Portfolio:** Maintain a diversified portfolio that aligns with your risk tolerance and goals. This reduces the impact of any single investment's performance.
- **Regular Reviews:** Periodically review your portfolio and rebalance as needed, rather than making changes based solely on recent performance.
- **Focus on Fundamentals:** Invest in companies and funds with strong fundamentals, regardless of their recent performance.

Example

A study by Dalbar showed that the average investor significantly underperforms the market due to poor timing decisions, often driven by chasing performance. Staying disciplined and focused on long-term goals can help avoid this pitfall.

Overlooking the Importance of Diversification

Diversification is a key strategy for managing risk. Overlooking its importance can lead to a portfolio that is too heavily weighted in one area, increasing vulnerability to market fluctuations.

Benefits of Diversification

- **Risk Reduction:** Spreading investments across different asset classes, sectors, and regions reduces exposure to any single investment's risk.
- **Smoother Returns:** A diversified portfolio is less likely to experience extreme volatility, providing more stable returns over time.
- **Growth Opportunities:** Diversification allows you to take advantage of growth opportunities in different markets and sectors.

How to Diversify

- **Asset Allocation:** Determine the right mix of stocks, bonds, real estate, and other assets based on your risk tolerance and goals.
- **Industry Diversification:** Invest in different industries to avoid overexposure to any single sector.
- **Geographic Diversification:** Spread your investments across different countries and regions to reduce exposure to economic and political risks in any single market.

Example

If your portfolio is heavily weighted in tech stocks, a downturn in the tech sector could significantly impact your investments. By diversifying across different industries, such as healthcare, finance, and consumer goods, you reduce the impact of any single sector's performance on your portfolio.

Summary

Avoiding common investment mistakes like emotional investing, timing the market, ignoring costs, chasing performance, and overlooking diversification can help you become a more disciplined and successful investor. By staying informed and focused on your long-term goals, you can build a solid foundation for financial success. In the next chapter, we'll explore advanced investment topics, including tax-advantaged accounts, real estate investing, and cryptocurrencies. Stay tuned!

Chapter 8: Advanced Topics

Once you've got the basics down, consider exploring these advanced topics to further enhance your investment strategy. In this chapter, we'll delve into tax-advantaged accounts, real estate investing, and investing in cryptocurrencies.

Tax-Advantaged Accounts

Tax-advantaged accounts offer benefits that can help your investments grow more efficiently by reducing or deferring taxes. Understanding how to utilize these accounts can significantly impact your overall returns.

Types of Tax-Advantaged Accounts

Individual Retirement Accounts (IRAs)

- **Traditional IRA:** Contributions are tax-deductible, and investments grow tax-deferred. You pay taxes on withdrawals in retirement.
- **Roth IRA:** Contributions are made with after-tax dollars, but investments grow tax-free. Withdrawals in retirement are also tax-free.

401(k) Plans

- Employer-sponsored retirement accounts with tax-deferred growth. Contributions are typically made pre-tax, reducing your taxable income. Some employers offer Roth 401(k) options, which are funded with after-tax dollars but grow tax-free.

Health Savings Accounts (HSAs)

- Available to individuals with high-deductible health plans. Contributions are tax-deductible, and withdrawals for qualified medical expenses are tax-free. HSAs can also be used as a supplemental retirement account due to their triple tax advantage.
- Health Savings Accounts (HSAs) are designed to help individuals save for future medical expenses. Contributions to an HSA are tax-deductible, and the money grows tax-free. However, there are a few considerations to keep in mind:
    - Contribution Limits: HSAs have annual contribution limits set by the IRS. For 2024, the limits are $3,850 for individuals and $7,750 for families. There's an additional $1,000 catch-up contribution allowed for those aged 55 or older.
    - Evaluating Medical Costs: If you overestimate how much you will use from your HSA in a given year, you may contribute more than necessary. Since unused HSA funds roll over year to year, over-contributing doesn't mean you lose the money, but it does mean that money is tied up in the HSA and cannot be used for non-medical expenses without penalties before age 65.
    - Non-Medical Withdrawals: Withdrawals for non-medical expenses before age 65 are subject to income tax and a 20% penalty. After age 65, non-medical withdrawals are subject to income tax but not the penalty.
    - Tax-Deferred Growth: While funds in an HSA grow tax-deferred, keeping an excessive balance for future medical expenses means those funds aren't available for other investments that might be more aligned with your overall financial strategy.
- Why It's Important to Evaluate Past Medical Costs:

- Predicting Future Expenses: By evaluating your recent past annual medical costs, you can make a more accurate estimate of how much you'll need to use from your HSA. This helps avoid over-contributing and ensures that you have enough liquidity for other financial needs.
- Optimal Contribution Strategy: Knowing your expected medical expenses allows you to contribute an appropriate amount to your HSA. You can maximize the tax benefits without locking away too much money in the account.
- Avoiding Penalties: By not overestimating your HSA usage, you can avoid unnecessary penalties and taxes on non-medical withdrawals.
- In summary, while HSAs offer significant tax advantages and are a great tool for managing healthcare costs, it's important to evaluate your recent past annual medical costs to avoid overestimating your needs and ensuring you contribute an appropriate amount.

529 College Savings Plans

- Designed for education savings. Contributions are made with after-tax dollars, but withdrawals for qualified education expenses are tax-free. Some states offer tax deductions or credits for contributions.

Benefits of Tax-Advantaged Accounts

- **Tax Deferral:** Investments grow without being taxed until withdrawal, allowing your money to compound more efficiently.
- **Tax-Free Growth:** In Roth accounts, your investments grow tax-free, providing significant tax savings over time.
- **Lower Taxable Income:** Contributions to traditional IRAs, 401(k)s, and HSAs can reduce your taxable income, potentially lowering your tax bracket.

How to Maximize Benefits

- **Maximize Contributions:** Contribute as much as you can to tax-advantaged accounts each year, up to the legal limits.
- **Employer Matching:** Take full advantage of any employer matching contributions in your 401(k). It's essentially free money.
- **Strategic Withdrawals:** Plan your withdrawals to minimize taxes. For example, consider withdrawing from Roth accounts during retirement to avoid higher tax brackets.

Examples

- If you contribute $6,000 annually to a Roth IRA starting at age 30, with an average annual return of 7%, you could have over $600,000 by age 65. All of this growth would be tax-free, providing substantial retirement income.
- If you contribute $6,000 annually to a Roth IRA starting at age 60, with an average annual return of 7%, you could have approximately $34,504.26 by age 65. This example illustrates that starting contributions later in life, such as at age 60, still benefits from compound interest, though the total growth is much less compared to starting earlier, like at age 30. If you have more years until retirement, the power of compound interest significantly increases the total value of your investments.

Real Estate Investing

Real estate can diversify your portfolio and provide passive income. You can invest directly in properties or through Real Estate Investment Trusts (REITs). Each option has its pros and cons, so research thoroughly before diving in.

Types of Real Estate Investments

- **Residential Properties:** Single-family homes, duplexes, or multi-family buildings that you can rent out to tenants. This provides rental income and potential appreciation.
- **Commercial Properties:** Office buildings, retail spaces, and industrial properties. These often require more capital and expertise but can offer higher returns.
- **REITs:** Companies that own and manage a portfolio of real estate properties. REITs are traded like stocks and provide regular dividends, offering an easy way to invest in real estate without owning physical properties.

Benefits of Real Estate Investing

- **Passive Income:** Rental properties can generate a steady stream of income.
- **Appreciation:** Properties can increase in value over time, providing capital gains when sold.
- **Diversification:** Real estate can reduce portfolio volatility by adding an asset class that doesn't always move in tandem with stocks and bonds.
- **Tax Advantages:** Real estate investments can offer tax benefits such as depreciation, mortgage interest deductions, and 1031 exchanges (which allow you to defer capital gains taxes[21] when swapping one investment property for another).

Challenges of Real Estate Investing

- **High Initial Capital:** Buying property requires significant upfront investment.
- **Management:** Owning rental properties involves maintenance, tenant management, and dealing with vacancies.

---

[21] https://www.investopedia.com/terms/c/capital_gains_tax.asp

- **Market Risk:** Real estate values can fluctuate based on economic conditions, interest rates, and local market trends.
- **Liquidity:** Real estate is less liquid than stocks or bonds, meaning it can take time to sell a property and access your funds.

How to Get Started

1. **Research the Market:** Understand local real estate trends, property values, and rental demand.
2. **Secure Financing:** Obtain a mortgage pre-approval if needed, and ensure you have enough capital for a down payment and closing costs.
3. **Start Small:** Consider starting with a single-family rental property to gain experience before moving on to larger investments.
4. **Consider REITs:** If you prefer a more hands-off approach, invest in REITs for exposure to real estate without the hassle of property management.

Example

If you buy a rental property for $200,000 with a 20% down payment, you'll need $40,000 upfront. If the property generates $1,500 per month in rent and your monthly expenses (mortgage, taxes, insurance, maintenance) are $1,200, you'll have a positive cash flow of $300 per month, or $3,600 per year. Over time, property appreciation and rental income can significantly boost your returns.

Investing in Cryptocurrencies

Cryptocurrencies are a relatively new and still quite volatile investment class. While they can offer high returns, they also come with significant risk. If you're interested in crypto, start with a small portion of your portfolio and educate yourself on the market.

What Are Cryptocurrencies?

Cryptocurrencies are digital or virtual currencies that use cryptography for security. They operate on decentralized networks based on blockchain technology[22], which ensures transparency and immutability[23]. Bitcoin, Ethereum, and Litecoin are some of the most well-known cryptocurrencies.

Benefits of Investing in Cryptocurrencies

- **High Return Potential:** Cryptocurrencies have experienced significant price increases, offering high potential returns.
- **Diversification:** Adding crypto to your portfolio can provide diversification benefits due to its low correlation with traditional asset classes.
- **Innovation and Adoption:** The growing acceptance of cryptocurrencies by businesses and institutions can drive future growth.

Risks of Investing in Cryptocurrencies

- **Volatility:** Cryptocurrency prices can be extremely volatile, leading to significant gains or losses in a short period.
- **Regulatory Risk:** Cryptocurrencies face regulatory uncertainty, and future regulations could impact their value and usability.
- **Security:** Cryptocurrencies are susceptible to hacking, scams, and technical issues. Proper security measures are crucial.

---

[22] https://www.investopedia.com/terms/b/blockchain.asp
[23] https://www.dictionary.com/browse/immutability

- **Lack of Fundamentals:** Unlike stocks or bonds, cryptocurrencies don't generate cash flow or dividends, making traditional valuation methods difficult.

How to Invest in Cryptocurrencies

1. **Educate Yourself:** Learn about blockchain technology, how cryptocurrencies work, and the factors that influence their prices.
2. **Choose a Platform:** Select a reputable cryptocurrency exchange to buy and sell crypto. Examples include Coinbase[24], Binance[25], and Kraken[26].
3. **Secure Your Investments:** Use hardware wallets[27] or secure online wallets to store your cryptocurrencies safely.
4. **Start Small:** Allocate a small portion of your portfolio to cryptocurrencies. Due to their high risk, it's wise to limit your exposure.
5. **Diversify:** Consider investing in a variety of cryptocurrencies to spread your risk. Research different projects and their potential use cases.

Example

If you invest $1,000 in Bitcoin and its price increases by 50%, your investment will grow to $1,500. However, due to its volatility, the price could also decrease significantly, so be prepared for potential losses.

Summary

Exploring advanced investment topics like tax-advantaged accounts, real estate investing, and cryptocurrencies can

---

[24] https://www.coinbase.com
[25] https://www.binance.com/en
[26] https://www.kraken.com/lp/platform
[27] https://crypto.com/university/what-is-a-hardware-wallet

enhance your overall strategy and provide additional growth opportunities. Each option comes with its own set of benefits and risks, so thorough research and careful consideration are essential. In the next chapter, we'll discuss how to stay informed about the investment world, continuing your education, and using resources and tools to your advantage. Stay tuned!

Chapter 9: Staying Informed

The investment world is always changing. Staying informed is key to success. In this chapter, we'll discuss how to continue your investment education, stay updated on market news, and use resources and tools to your advantage.

Continuing Your Investment Education

Investing is a lifelong learning process. The more you know, the better decisions you can make. Here are some ways to keep learning:

Books

- "The Intelligent Investor" by Benjamin Graham[28]: A classic book on value investing, offering timeless advice on investment principles and strategies.
- "A Random Walk Down Wall Street" by Burton Malkiel[29]: An accessible introduction to investing, covering various investment strategies and the importance of diversification.
- "Common Stocks and Uncommon Profits" by Philip Fisher[30]: Insights into growth investing and how to analyze companies for long-term investment.

---

[28] https://amzn.to/3VUqt47
[29] https://amzn.to/4eO2I6q
[30] https://amzn.to/3WcYf68

Courses and Workshops

- **Online Courses:** Platforms like Coursera[31], Udemy[32], and Khan Academy[33] offer courses on investing, personal finance, and financial markets.
- **Financial Workshops:** Many financial institutions and community organizations offer free or low-cost workshops on investing and financial planning.

Podcasts

- "The Investor's Podcast Network"[34]: A series of podcasts covering various investment topics, including stock investing, personal finance, and market analysis.
- "BiggerPockets Real Estate Podcast"[35]: Focuses on real estate investing, with interviews and tips from experienced investors.
- "Money for the Rest of Us"[36]: Discusses a broad range of investment topics, helping listeners understand how the financial world works.

Newsletters and Blogs

- Morningstar[37]: Provides research, analysis, and insights on mutual funds, stocks, and other investments.

---

[31] https://www.coursera.org/specializations/investment-portolio-management

[32] https://www.udemy.com/topic/investing

[33] https://www.khanacademy.org/college-careers-more/financial-literacy/xa6995ea67a8e9fdd:investments-retirement/xa6995ea67a8e9fdd:saving-and-investing

[34] https://www.theinvestorspodcast.com

[35] https://www.biggerpockets.com/podcasts/real-estate

[36] https://moneyfortherestofus.com/episodes

[37] https://investor.morningstar.com/mm/learn

- Seeking Alpha[38]: A platform where investors share their analyses and opinions on various stocks and investment strategies.
- The Motley Fool[39]: Offers articles, podcasts, and newsletters on investing and personal finance.

Resources and Tools

Utilizing the right resources and tools can help you stay informed and make better investment decisions.

Financial News Websites

- Bloomberg[40]: Offers comprehensive news and analysis on financial markets, companies, and global economies.
- CNBC[41]: Provides up-to-date market news, stock quotes, and financial advice.
- Reuters[42]: Delivers international news coverage, including financial and market reports.

Investment Research Tools

- Yahoo Finance[43]: A free resource for stock quotes, financial news, and investment research.
- Morningstar[44]: Offers detailed analysis, ratings, and research on stocks, mutual funds, and ETFs.
- Seeking Alpha: Provides crowd-sourced investment research, articles, and market analysis.

---

[38] https://seekingalpha.com
[39] https://www.fool.com
[40] https://www.bloomberg.com
[41] https://www.cnbc.com/finance
[42] https://www.reuters.com/business/finance
[43] https://finance.yahoo.com
[44] https://investor.morningstar.com/mm/learn

Portfolio Management Tools

- Empower[45]: A comprehensive financial tool that helps you track your investments, manage your portfolio, and plan for retirement.
- Tiller Money[46]: A budgeting tool that also offers basic investment tracking and financial planning features.
- Quicken[47]: A financial management tool that helps you track spending, manage investments, and plan for the future.

Following the Market News

Staying updated on market news helps you understand the factors influencing your investments and make timely decisions. Here are some tips for keeping up with the market:

- **Set Up Alerts:** Use financial news websites and apps to set up alerts for news and updates on your investments and areas of interest.
- **Daily Reviews:** Spend a few minutes each day reviewing market news and updates. This helps you stay informed without feeling overwhelmed.
- **Weekly Summaries:** Read weekly market summaries to get an overview of major events and trends that occurred during the week.

Example

If you invest in a particular sector, such as technology, setting up alerts for news related to major tech companies and trends can help you stay ahead of significant developments that might impact your investments.

---

[45] https://www.empower.com/empower-personal-wealth-transition
[46] https://www.tillerhq.com
[47] https://www.quicken.com

Engage with Financial Communities

Joining investment communities, both online and offline, can provide valuable insights and support. You can learn from the experiences of others and share your own knowledge.

- **Online Forums:** Websites like Reddit (r/investing, r/personalfinance) and Bogleheads offer active communities discussing various investment topics.
- **Local Investment Clubs:** Consider joining or forming a local investment club where members pool their knowledge and resources to make collective investment decisions.

Attend Conferences and Seminars

Investment conferences and seminars provide opportunities to hear from industry experts, network with other investors, and learn about the latest trends and strategies.

- [Financial Planning Association (FPA) Conferences][48]: Offer educational sessions, workshops, and networking opportunities for financial professionals and investors.
- [MoneyShow][49]: Hosts investment conferences in various cities, featuring presentations from market experts, panel discussions, and workshops.

Mentorship and Professional Advice

Seeking mentorship from experienced investors or working with a financial advisor can provide personalized guidance and accelerate your learning curve.

---

[48] https://conference.financial-planning.com/event/advise-ai/summary
[49] https://www.moneyshow.com

- **Mentorship Programs:** Some financial organizations and community groups offer mentorship programs connecting novice investors with experienced mentors.
- **Certified Financial Planners (CFPs):** Working with a CFP can help you develop a comprehensive financial plan and receive tailored investment advice.

Summary

Staying informed and continuing your investment education is crucial for long-term success. Utilize books, courses, podcasts, newsletters, and financial news websites to keep learning. Leverage investment research tools, portfolio management tools, and set up alerts to stay updated on market news. Engaging with financial communities, attending conferences, and seeking mentorship can further enhance your knowledge and decision-making skills. In the final chapter, we'll recap the key points and offer some encouragement for your future as an investor. Stay tuned!

Chapter 10: Conclusion

Congratulations! You've made it through the essentials of investing for beginners. By now, you should have a solid understanding of why investing matters, how to get started, the basics of different investment types, building and managing your portfolio, various investment strategies, common mistakes to avoid, advanced investment topics, and how to stay informed. In this final chapter, we'll recap the key points and offer some encouragement for your future as an investor.

Recap of Key Points

Chapter 1: Introduction

- **Why Investing Matters:** Investing helps you build wealth, beat inflation, achieve financial goals, and ensure financial security.
- **Personal Journey:** Understanding the significance of starting early and learning from experiences can guide you on your investment journey.

Chapter 2: Getting Started

- **Understanding Your Financial Situation:** Creating a budget and knowing your income, expenses, and debts is crucial.
- **Setting Financial Goals:** Clear, specific, and measurable goals help shape your investment strategy.
- **Compound Interest:** Start early to take advantage of compound interest, where your returns earn returns over time.

Chapter 3: Investment Basics

- **Stocks and Bonds:** Stocks offer high returns but higher risk, while bonds provide stability and lower returns.
- **Risk vs. Reward:** Balancing risk and reward based on your risk tolerance and goals is essential.
- **Diversification:** Spreading investments across different asset classes reduces risk and stabilizes returns.

Chapter 4: How to Invest

- **Opening an Investment Account:** Choose the right type of account (brokerage, retirement) and a reputable brokerage.
- **DIY vs. Financial Advisors:** Decide between managing your investments yourself or hiring an advisor.
- **Understanding Investment Fees:** Minimize costs to maximize your returns by choosing low-cost funds and avoiding frequent trading.

Chapter 5: Building Your Portfolio

- **Asset Allocation:** Determine the right mix of stocks, bonds, real estate, and other assets.
- **Rebalancing:** Regularly adjust your portfolio to maintain your target allocation.
- **Long-term vs. Short-term Investments:** Balance investments based on your time horizon and goals.

Chapter 6: Investment Strategies

- **Value Investing:** Buy undervalued stocks with strong fundamentals.
- **Growth Investing:** Focus on companies with high growth potential.

- **Dividend Investing:** Invest in companies that pay regular dividends for a steady income stream.

Chapter 7: Common Investment Mistakes

- **Emotional Investing:** Avoid making decisions based on fear or greed.
- **Timing the Market:** Focus on long-term investing rather than trying to predict market movements.
- **Ignoring Costs:** Pay attention to investment fees and taxes to maximize returns.
- **Chasing Performance:** Stick to your investment strategy instead of following the latest hot stock.

Chapter 8: Advanced Topics

- **Tax-Advantaged Accounts:** Use accounts like IRAs, 401(k)s, HSAs, and 529 plans to reduce or defer taxes.
- **Real Estate Investing:** Diversify your portfolio with rental properties or REITs.
- **Cryptocurrencies:** Invest cautiously in this volatile asset class, starting with a small portion of your portfolio.

Chapter 9: Staying Informed

- **Continuing Education:** Read books, take courses, listen to podcasts, and engage with financial communities.
- **Resources and Tools:** Use financial news websites, investment research tools, and portfolio management tools.
- **Following the Market:** Stay updated on market news and developments to make informed decisions.

Encouragement for the Future

Investing can seem daunting at first, but remember, it's a journey, not a sprint. Here are some final tips and encouragement as you continue your investment journey:

- **Stay Patient:** Investing is a long-term game. Stay patient and avoid making hasty decisions based on short-term market movements.
- **Keep Learning:** The investment world is constantly evolving. Stay curious and keep learning to adapt to new trends and opportunities.
- **Stay Disciplined:** Stick to your investment plan, rebalance your portfolio regularly, and avoid letting emotions drive your decisions.
- **Seek Support:** Don't hesitate to seek advice from financial professionals or join investment communities to share experiences and learn from others.
- **Celebrate Milestones:** Recognize and celebrate your progress. Every step you take towards your financial goals is an achievement.

Remember, the key to successful investing is not about timing the market but time in the market. Stay focused on your long-term goals, diversify your investments, and let the power of compounding work for you. You've got this!

That concludes our journey through "Investing for Beginners." I hope this guide has provided you with the knowledge and confidence to embark on your investment journey. Here's to your financial success!

Appendix: Beginner-Friendly Investment Sites and Tools

Navigating the world of investing can be easier with the right tools and platforms. Here are some beginner-friendly investment sites and tools to help you get started:

Investment Platforms

Stash

Stash (*stash.com*) is an easy-to-use investment app that helps beginners start investing with as little as $5. It offers personalized advice and educational resources to help you build your portfolio.

Acorns

Acorns (*acorns.com*) rounds up your everyday purchases to the nearest dollar and invests the spare change. It's a great way to start investing without thinking about it.

Robinhood

Robinhood (*robinhood.com*) offers commission-free trading of stocks, ETFs, options, and cryptocurrencies. Its user-friendly interface makes it ideal for beginners.

Betterment

Betterment (*betterment.com*) is a robo-advisor that creates a diversified portfolio for you based on your goals and risk tolerance. It also offers retirement planning and other financial advice.

Wealthfront

Wealthfront (*wealthfront.com*) is another robo-advisor that provides automated investment management and financial planning tools. It's known for its tax-efficient strategies and low fees.

Vanguard

Vanguard (*vanguard.com*) offers a range of low-cost mutual funds and ETFs. It's a favorite among long-term investors looking for cost-effective investment options.

Fidelity

Fidelity (*fidelity.com*) provides a wide array of investment options, including stocks, bonds, mutual funds, and ETFs. It also offers extensive research tools and educational resources.

Financial News and Research Tools

Morningstar

Morningstar (*morningstar.com*) offers in-depth research, analysis, and ratings on stocks, mutual funds, and ETFs. It's a valuable resource for making informed investment decisions.

Yahoo Finance

Yahoo Finance (*finance.yahoo.com*) provides stock quotes, financial news, and data. It's a comprehensive tool for tracking market movements and researching investments.

Seeking Alpha

Seeking Alpha (*seekingalpha.com*) features investment research and analysis from a community of investors. It covers a wide range of asset classes and investment strategies.

Educational Resources

Investopedia

Investopedia (*investopedia*) offers a wealth of information on investing, including tutorials, articles, and a comprehensive financial dictionary.

Khan Academy – Personal Finance

Khan Academy (*khanacademy.org*) provides free courses on personal finance and investing, making complex topics accessible and easy to understand.

Coursera

Coursera (*coursera.org*) offers online courses on investing, finance, and economics from top universities and institutions. It's a great way to deepen your knowledge.

The Motley Fool

The Motley Fool (*fool.com*) provides investment advice, stock recommendations, and financial education through articles, podcasts, and newsletters.

NerdWallet

NerdWallet (*nerdwallet.com*) offers financial tools and advice on investing, credit cards, loans, and more. It's a useful resource for managing your finances.

Budgeting and Financial Planning Tools

Tiller Money

Tiller Money (*tillerhq.com*) is a free budgeting tool that helps you track spending, create budgets, and manage your finances. It also provides basic investment tracking features.

Personal Capital

Empower (*empower.com*) offers free financial tools to track your investments, plan for retirement, and manage your entire financial picture.

YNAB (You Need A Budget)

YNAB (*ynab.com*) is a popular budgeting app that helps you take control of your money and plan for future expenses.

These resources can help you start your investment journey, stay informed, and make educated decisions. Remember, the key to successful investing is continuous learning and staying updated with the latest market trends and strategies.

Index

A
- Asset Allocation, 27
    - Example Portfolios, 28
    - Adjusting Over Time, 29

B
- Bonds, 15
    - Benefits, 16
    - Risks, 17
    - Rewards, 17

C
- Compound Interest, 12
- Costs
    - Ignoring Impact, 43
    - Types, 43
    - How to Minimize, 44
- Cryptocurrencies, 54
    - Benefits, 55
    - Risks, 55
    - How to Invest, 56

D
- Diversification, 18, 46
    - Benefits, 18, 42, 46
    - How to Diversify, 18, 46

E
- Education
    - Books, 59
    - Courses and Workshops, 60
    - Podcasts, 60
    - Newsletters and Blogs, 60
    - Resources and Tools, 61
    - Market News, 62
    - Communities, 63
    - Conferences and Seminars, 63
    - Mentorship and Advice, 63

- EFTs, 16
- Emotional Investing
  - Traps, 41
  - How to Avoid, 41
- Expense Ratios, 25
  - Types of Costs, 42
  - Importance of Minimizing, 43

F

- Financial Goals
  - Setting, 12
  - Taking Action, 13

G

- Growth Investing, 36
  - Key Principles, 37
  - How to Implement, 37

H

- Health Savings Accounts (HSAs)
  - Contribution Limits, 50
  - Non-Medical Withdrawals, 50
  - Evaluating Medical Costs, 50
  - Tax-Deferred Growth, 50

I

- Investing
  - Why it Matters, 7
  - Personal Story, 8
  - Personal Lessons Learned, 8
- Investment Accounts
  - Types of Accounts, 21
  - Choosing a Brokerage, 22
  - Opening an Account, 22
  - DIY, 23
  - Financial Advisors, 24
  - Fees, 25
- Investment Basics
  - Stocks, 15
  - Bonds, 15

    - Other Types, 16
    - Risk vs. Reward, 16
    - Diversification, 18
- Intrinsic Value, 35

L
- Long-term Investments, 32

M
- Margin of Safety, 35
- Mutual Funds, 16

O
- Overconfidence, 41
    - How to Manage, 42

P
- Performance
    - Chasing Mistake, 45
    - Better Approaches, 45
- Portfolio Management
    - Asset Classes, 27
    - Allocation, 28
    - Rebalancing, 29

R
- Rebalancing, 29
    - Why Rebalance, 29
    - How to Rebalance, 30
- Real Estate Investing, 52
    - Types, 53
    - Benefits, 53
    - Challenges, 53
    - How to Get Started, 54

S
- Short-term Investments, 32
- Sites and Tools
    - Platforms, 69
    - Educational Resources, 71
    - Budget and Financial Planning Tools, 72
- Stocks, 15

- Benefits, 15
- Risks, 16
- Rewards, 17
- Strategies
  - Value Investing, 35
  - Growth Investing, 36
  - Dividend Investing, 38
  - Combining Strategies, 39
- Summary
  - Key Points Recap, 65
  - Encouragement for Future, 68

T

- Tax-Advantaged Accounts
  - IRAs, 49
  - 401(k)s, 49
  - HSAs, 50
  - 529 College Savings, 51
  - Benefits, 51
  - How to Maximize, 52
- Timing the Market
  - Why It Fails, 42
  - Better Strategies, 43

U

- Understanding Your Financial Situation
  - How to Assess, 11
  - Taking Action, 13

V

- Value Investing
  - Key Principles, 35
  - How to Implement, 36

www.ingramcontent.com/pod-product-compliance
Lightning Source LLC
Chambersburg PA
CBHW071842210526
45479CB00001B/244